MW00342296

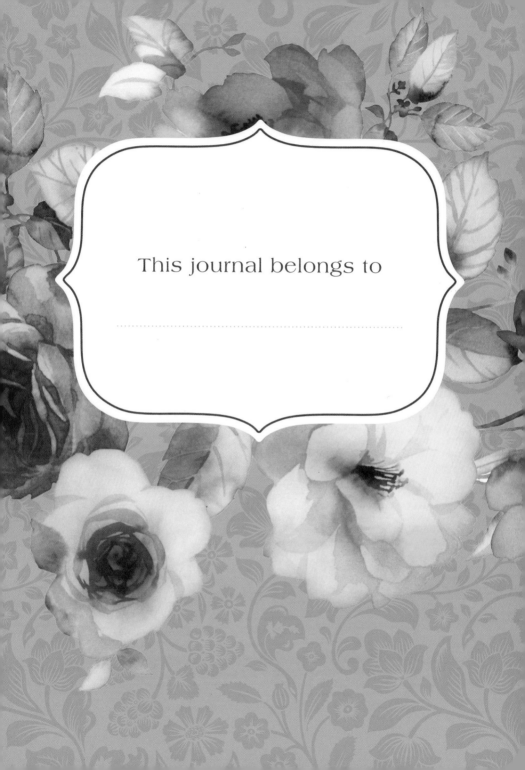

This journal belongs to

....

© 2017 by Barbour Publishing, Inc.

Compiled by Linda Hang.

Print ISBN 978-1-68322-101-2

All poems © Helen Steiner Rice Foundation Fund, LLC, a wholly owned subsidary of Cincinnati Museum Center. All rights reserved.

All rights reserved. No part of this publication may be reproduced or transmitted for commercial purposes, except for brief quotations in printed reviews, without written permission of the publisher.

Devotional (non-poetry) text appeared in *A Celebration of Love, A Celebration of God's Love, A Celebration of Friendship, A Celebration of Family,* written by Snapdragon Group™ Tulsa, Oklahoma, USA.

All scripture quotations are taken from the King James Version of the Bible.

Published by Barbour Books, an imprint of Barbour Publishing, Inc., P.O. Box 719, Uhrichsville, Ohio 44683, www.barbourbooks.com

Our mission is to publish and distribute inspirational products offering exceptional value and biblical encouragement to the masses.

ecpa Member of the Evangelical Christian Publishers Association

Printed in China.

Helen Steiner Rice

Reflections
for
*Each
New Day*

JOURNAL

BARBOUR BOOKS
An Imprint of Barbour Publishing, Inc.

Introduction

Each day of life is a gift from our Father God—a new opportunity to reflect on His goodness, His mercy, His blessings. . .His never-ending love for us. Our great Creator, almighty God, looks down on us and chooses to see us with loving eyes, call us His children, and redeem us by His grace. We may never understand it; but we can accept and celebrate it.

That's exactly what this beautiful journal is designed to do. As you read through and journal alongside the beautiful, simple, and insightful poetry of Helen Steiner Rice, we pray you will be blessed and inspired to pen your own words—be it poetry or prose. Sprinkled throughout you'll also find several devotional thoughts designed to draw you into a deeper reflection of life's good gifts.

Every good gift and
every perfect gift is from above,
and cometh down from the Father of lights,
with whom is no variableness,
neither shadow of turning.
JAMES 1:17

My God Is No Stranger

I've never seen God,
but I know how I feel—
It's people like you
who make Him so real.
My God is no stranger—
He's so friendly each day,
And He doesn't ask me
to weep when I pray.
It seems that I pass Him
so often each day
In the faces of people
I meet on my way. . .
I wish I might meet Him
much more than I do—
I wish that there were
more people like you.

–HSR

A Friend Is a Gift from God

Among the great and glorious gifts
our heavenly Father sends
Is the gift of understanding
that we find in loving friends. . .
For in this world of trouble that is filled with anxious care,
Everybody needs a friend in whom they're free to share
The little secret heartaches that lay heavy on the mind—
Not just a mere acquaintance
but someone who's just our kind. . .
For somehow in the generous heart
of loving, faithful friends,
The good God in His charity and wisdom always sends
A sense of understanding and the power of perception
And mixes these fine qualities
with kindness and affection. . .
So when we need some sympathy
or a friendly hand to touch
Or one who listens and speaks words that mean so much,
We seek a true and trusted friend
in the knowledge that we'll find
A heart that's sympathetic and an understanding mind. . .
And often just without a word there seems to be a union
Of thoughts and kindred feelings,
for God gives true friends communion.

–HSR

The Gift of Friendship

Friendship is a priceless gift
that cannot be bought or sold
But its value is far greater
than a mountain made of gold—
For gold is cold and lifeless,
it can neither see nor hear,
And in the time of trouble
it is powerless to cheer.
It has no ears to listen,
no heart to understand,
It cannot bring you comfort
or reach out a helping hand—
So when you ask God for a gift,
be thankful if He sends
Not diamonds, pearls, or riches,
but the love of real true friends.

–HSR

Hope in Friendship

*So many things
in the line of duty
Drain us of effort
and leave us no beauty,
And the dust of the soul
grows thick and unswept;
The spirit is drenched
in tears unwept.
But just as we fall
beside the road,
Discouraged with life
and bowed down with our load,
We lift our eyes,
and what seemed a dead end
Is the street of dreams
where we meet a friend.*

–HSR

Life Is a Garden

Life is a garden,
good friends are the flowers,
And times spent together
life's happiest hours. . .
And friendship, like flowers,
blooms ever more fair
When carefully tended
by dear friends who care. . .
And life's lovely garden
would be sweeter by far
If all who passed through it
were as nice as you are.

–HSR

The Golden Chain of Friendship

Friendship is a golden chain,
the links are friends so dear,
And like a rare and precious jewel,
it's treasured more each year.
It's clasped together firmly
with a love that's deep and true,
And it's rich with happy memories
and fond recollections, too.
Time can't destroy its beauty,
for as long as memory lives,
Years can't erase the pleasure
that the joy of friendship gives.
For friendship is a priceless gift
that can't be bought or sold,
And to have an understanding friend
is worth far more than gold.
And the golden chain of friendship
is a strong and blessed tie
Binding kindred hearts together
as the years go passing by.

–HSR

Faces in the Crowd

But to the saints that are in the earth,
and to the excellent, in whom is all my delight.
PSALM 16:3

Have you ever stopped to imagine how many people cross your path in the course of a year? Not just the ones you recognize or even the ones you notice, but all the people you encounter? The young mother who passes you in the supermarket aisle with her two little ones in tow. Or the woman sitting in the next chair at the hair salon, casting a timid smile your way. How about the man who delivers your mail or fixes your car or briefly passes you on the street? The number is probably astronomical. Most of these chance encounters are easily forgotten within a few moments—if remembered at all.

But now and then you look up and see instant recognition in the eyes of a stranger. Soon that stranger becomes a friend. What makes that person stand out from the teeming sea of people you pass by each day? The answer could well be the hand of God.

Our God is a friendly God: kind, loving, and generous. He's always there for us when we need Him. He is the personification of friendship. Is it so hard to believe, then, that God takes time to point out those special faces in the crowd to us? That He chooses our friends for us?

Begin to think of your friends as an expression of God's love for you—His remarkable gifts—because that's exactly what they are!

Help Us to See and Understand

God, give us wider vision to see and understand
That both the sunshine and the showers
are gifts from Thy great hand,
And when our lives are overcast
with trouble and with care,
Give us faith to see beyond the dark clouds of despair,
And give us strength to rise above
the mist of doubt and fear
And recognize the hidden smile
behind each burning tear. . .
And teach us that it takes the showers
to make the flowers grow,
And only in the storms of life
when the winds of trouble blow
Can man, too, reach maturity
and grow in faith and grace
And gain the strength and courage to enable him to face
Sunny days as well as rain, high peaks as well as low,
Knowing that the April showers
will make May flowers grow. . .
And then at last may we accept
the sunshine and the showers,
Confident it takes them both
to make salvation ours.

–HSR

"In Him We Live and Move and Have Our Being"

We walk in a world that is strange and unknown,
And in the midst of the crowd we still feel alone.
We question our purpose, our part, and our place
In this vast land of mystery suspended in space.
We probe and explore and try hard to explain
The tumult of thoughts that our minds entertain,
But all of our problems and complex explanations
Of man's inner feelings and fears and frustrations
Still leave us engulfed in the mystery of life
With all of its struggles and suffering and strife,
Unable to fathom what tomorrow will bring—
But there is one truth to which we can cling. . .
For while life's a mystery man can't understand,
The great Giver of life is holding our hands,
And safe in His care there is no need for seeing,
"For in Him we live and move and have our being."

–HSR

God Already Knows

Beyond that which words can interpret
or theology can explain
The world feels a shower of refreshment
that falls like the gentle rain
On hearts that are parched with problems
and are searching to find the way
To somehow attract God's attention
through well-chosen words as they pray,
Not knowing that God in His wisdom
can sense all man's worry and woe,
For there is nothing man can conceal
that God does not already know. . .
So kneel in prayer in His presence
and you'll find no need to speak,
For softly in silent communion
God grants you the peace that you seek.

–HSR

The Way to Love and Peace

Let us recognize we're facing
problems man has never solved,
And with all our daily efforts
life grows more and more involved. . .
But our future will seem brighter,
and we'll meet with less resistance
If we call upon our Father
and seek divine assistance.
For the spirit can unravel
many tangled, knotted threads
That defy the skill and power
of the world's best hands and heads,
And our plans for growth and progress,
of which we all have dreamed,
Cannot survive materially
unless our spirits are redeemed. . .
For only when the mind of man
is united with the soul
Can love and peace combine to make
our lives complete and whole.

–HSR

Finding Faith in a Flower

Sometimes when faith is running low
And I cannot fathom why things are so,
I walk among the flowers that grow
And learn the answers to all I would know. . .
For among my flowers I have come to see
Life's miracle and its mystery,
And standing in silence and reverie,
My faith comes flooding back to me.

–HSR

Wisdom, My Sister

Say unto wisdom, Thou art my sister;
and call understanding thy kinswoman.
PROVERBS 7:4

A sister knows how to encourage you when you are down. A sister loves you with a special love. She can give advice and teach you much about the challenges of life, yet she is able to call out the best characteristics in you. What, then, would it be like to call Wisdom your sister—to draw her so close that you could live with her continual guidance?

Solomon, considered to be the wisest man ever to live, called wisdom the principal thing a person should seek to obtain. He advises you to embrace her, to hold on to her, just as you would a trustworthy sibling.

Sisters are better than friends. They aren't afraid to tell you the difficult truth and challenge you to move forward in the face of hardship and trouble. In the same way, wisdom won't coddle you. It will call you to action, back you up, teach you to be honest and faithful, and help you be your best in every situation.

If you grew up with a good sister, you are blessed. You probably found her to be a trusted confidant, protector, and advocate. Wisdom can be trusted as well. It will inspire you and provide you with courage and strength. Whatever circumstances you may face, treat wisdom like a sister!

Springtime Glory

Flowers buried beneath the snow
Awakening again to live and grow—
Leaves that fell to the earth to die
Enriching the soil in which they lie—
Lifeless-looking, stark, stripped trees
Bursting with buds in the springtime breeze
Are just a few examples of
The greatness of God's power and love,
And in this blaze of springtime glory,
Just who could doubt the Easter story!

–HSR

Reflections of God's Face

The silent stars in timeless skies,
The wonderment in children's eyes,
The autumn haze, the breath of spring,
The chirping song the crickets sing,
A rosebud in a slender vase
Are all reflections of God's face.

–HSR

God Is No Stranger

God is no stranger in a faraway place—
He's as close as the wind that blows 'cross my face.
It's true I can't see the wind as it blows,
But I feel it around me and my heart surely knows
That God's mighty hand can be felt everywhere,
For there's nothing on earth that is not in God's care.
The sky and the stars, the waves and the sea,
The dew on the grass, the leaves on a tree
Are constant reminders of God and His nearness
Proclaiming His presence with crystal-like clearness.
So how could I think God was far, far away
When I feel Him beside me every hour of the day?
And I've plenty of reasons to know God's my friend,
And this is one friendship that time cannot end.

–HSR

The Hand of God Is Everywhere

It's true we have never looked on His face,
But His likeness shines forth from every place,
For the hand of God is everywhere
Along life's busy thoroughfare,
And His presence can be felt and seen
Right in the midst of our daily routine.
Things we touch and see and feel
Are what make God so very real.

–HSR

His Likeness Shines Forth

In everything both great and small
We see the hand of God in all,
And every day, somewhere, someplace,
We see the likeness of His face.
For who can watch a new day's birth
Or touch the warm, life-giving earth
Or feel the softness of a breeze
Or look at skies through lacy trees
And say they've never seen His face
Or looked upon His throne of grace.
And man's search for God will end and begin
When he opens his heart to let Christ in.

–HSR

This Is My Father's World

Everywhere across the land
You see God's face and touch His hand
Each time you look up in the sky
Or watch the fluffy clouds drift by,
Or feel the sunshine, warm and bright,
Or watch the dark night turn to light,
Or hear a bluebird brightly sing,
Or see the winter turn to spring,
Or stop to pick a daffodil,
Or gather violets on some hill,
Or touch a leaf or see a tree,
It's all God whispering, "This is Me.
And I am faith and I am light,
And in Me there shall be no night."

–HSR

The Web of Life

The spider taketh hold with her hands,
and is in kings' palaces.

PROVERBS 30:28

A trip out early on a misty morning seems otherworldly. Things feel and look different in the first light of dawn. The white circles of a spider's web in the dewy grass along the roadside look like patches of frost. Frost on such a morning is nonexistent, but every web shows up when it is heavy with dew and lit with the silvery light of early morning. How many webs fill the fence's spaces and run from signpost to tree branch! How many webs show up along the tall tufts of grass and stretch to the stems of wildflowers! The landscape looks covered with a jumble of lace pieces freshly washed and laid out to dry.

The webs are alike, and yet each one is different. Each is crafted by a tiny spider—woven of the silk filigree its body produces. Each work of art is a trap to catch breakfast from the air.

Even if you have never opened a Bible or heard the message of God's great love for you, He has written love messages to you everywhere you look. Even if you have not been aware of His majesty and power, seeing the world awaken in the early light and inspecting the impossibility of a silvery spider's web should be enough to tell you that God is real and wants to be part of your life.

God's Messengers

The unexpected kindness
from an unexpected place,
A hand outstretched in friendship,
a smile on someone's face,
A word of understanding
spoken in a time of trial
Are unexpected miracles
that make life more worthwhile.
We know not how it happened
that in an hour of need
Somebody out of nowhere
proved to be a friend indeed. . .
For God has many messengers
we fail to recognize,
But He sends them when we need them,
and His ways are wondrous and wise. . .
So keep looking for an angel
and keep listening to hear,
For on life's busy, crowded streets,
you will find God's presence near.

–HSR

Count Your Gains, Not Your Losses

As we travel down life's busy road
Complaining of our heavy load,
We often think God's been unfair
And given us much more than our share
Of daily little irritations
And disappointing tribulations.
We're discontented with our lot
And all the bad breaks that we got.
We count our losses, not our gain,
And remember only tears and pain.
The good things we forget completely—
When God looked down and blessed us sweetly.
Our troubles fill our every thought—
We dwell upon the goals we sought,
And wrapped up in our own despair,
We have no time to see or share
Another's load that far outweighs
Our little problems and dismays. . .
And so we walk with heads held low,
And little do we guess or know
That someone near us on life's street
Is burdened deeply with defeat,
And if we'd but forget our care
And stop in sympathy to share
The burden that our brother carried,
Our minds and hearts would be less harried
And we would feel our load was small—
In fact, we carried no load at all.

–HSR

The Fragrance Remains

There's an old Chinese proverb that if practiced each day
Would change the whole world in a wonderful way.
Its truth is so simple, it's easy to do,
And it works every time and successfully, too.
For you can't do a kindness without a reward—
Not in silver nor gold but in joy from the Lord.
You can't light a candle to show others the way
Without feeling the warmth of that bright little ray,
And you can't pluck a rose all fragrant with dew
Without part of its fragrance remaining with you.

–HSR

Take Time to Be Kind

Kindness is a virtue
given by the Lord—
It pays dividends in happiness
and joy is its reward.
For if you practice kindness
in all you say and do,
The Lord will wrap His kindness
around your heart and you.

–HSR

In His Footsteps

When someone does a kindness,
it always seems to me
That's the way God up in heaven
would like us all to be.
For when we bring some pleasure
to another human heart,
We have followed in His footsteps,
and we've had a little part
In serving God who loves us
for I'm very sure it's true
That in serving those around us,
we serve and please God, too.

–HSR

Conscious Acts of Kindness

Thus speaketh the LORD of hosts, saying,
Execute true judgment, and shew mercy
and compassions every man to his brother.
ZECHARIAH 7:9

Kindness doesn't happen by accident. It is a conscious action, and that's what makes it so special. Think of it this way: The sun doesn't come up each morning as an act of kindness to human beings. God created it and set it in motion on a specific path. It simply does what it was created to do—provide light and heat to the solar system. But human beings have the gift of conscious intent. We can choose to do a thing and then carry it out. That makes us uniquely capable of initiating kind acts and speaking kind words.

When someone does something for us—something unexpected and unearned—it tells us that we are not alone on the road of life. What a sweet relief that is! Then as kindnesses are exchanged, we begin to understand that we were meant to be there for each other, and friendship ultimately blossoms.

You were meant to be kind, but unlike the sun, you have been given the gift to choose your own course. That smile, those kind words, the favor someone needs—none of that will happen unless you decide to make it happen. You have the ability to bless others and simultaneously bless yourself as a result.

Spend some time today considering ways to initiate kindness. Lighten someone's burden, cheer someone's day, or lend a hand. Then stand back and watch friendship grow.

A Sure Way to a Happy Day

Happiness is something we create in our minds—
It's not something you search for and so seldom find.
It's just waking up and beginning the day
By counting our blessings and kneeling to pray.
It's giving up thoughts that breed discontent
And accepting what comes as a gift heaven-sent.
It's giving up wishing for things we have not
And making the best of whatever we've got.
It's knowing that life is determined for us
And pursuing our tasks without fret, fume, or fuss. . .
For it's by completing what God gives us to do
That we find real contentment and happiness, too.

–HSR

Three Treasures

There are three treasures
More priceless than gold.
For if you possess them
You've riches untold—
For with faith to believe
What your eyes cannot see,
And hope to look forward
To joy yet to be,
And love to transform
The most commonplace
Into beauty and kindness
And goodness and grace,
There's nothing too much
To accomplish or do.
For with faith, hope, and love
To carry you through,
Your life will be happy
And full and complete.
For with faith, hope, and love
The bitter turns sweet.

–HSR

Heart Gifts

It's not the things that can be bought
That are life's richest treasures;
It's just the little "heart gifts"
That money cannot measure—
A cheerful smile, a friendly word,
A sympathetic nod,
All priceless little treasures
From the storehouse of our God—
They are the things that can't be bought
With silver or with gold,
For thoughtfulness and kindness
And love are never sold—
They are the priceless things in life
For which no one can pay,
And the giver finds rich recompense
In giving them away.

—HSR

The Richest Gifts

The richest gifts
Are God's to give.
As long as you live,
May you walk with Him
And dwell in His love
As He sends you good gifts
From heaven above.

–HSR

God's Jewels

We watch the rich and famous
bedecked in precious jewels,
Enjoying earthly pleasures,
defying moral rules,
And in our mood of discontent
we sink into despair
And long for earthly riches
and feel cheated of our share. . .
But stop these idle musings.
God has stored up for you
Treasures that are far beyond
earth's jewels and riches, too.
For never, never discount
what God has promised man
If he will walk in meekness
and accept God's flawless plan.
For if we heed His teaching
as we journey through the years,
We'll find the richest jewels of all
are crystallized from tears.

–HSR

The Riches of Love

For where your treasure is,
there will your heart be also.

LUKE 12:34

If we don't see them all around us, we see them on television—people who seem to have so much more than we do! They buy expensive clothes from designer boutiques while we balk at the price of a sweater at the local department store. They go on exotic vacations while we count our pennies to save up for a weekend away. It doesn't seem fair, does it?

Feelings of discontent come to everyone from time to time. When you are bothered by these thoughts, God invites you to bring your concerns to Him. It's okay to tell Him exactly what you believe you are missing and to be specific about what is causing you so much unhappiness. Then let go of these things, and let God's Spirit take over.

The Holy Spirit has the power to open your eyes to the riches God has poured on you. In Him, you are robed in saving faith, covered with His promises, and adorned with an eternal relationship with your heavenly Father. Even the wealthiest people in the world could not buy this for themselves! But to you it has been freely given, because God chose to lavish on you the riches of His love—your true and lasting treasure.

Memories

*Tender little memories
Of some word or deed
Give us strength and courage
When we are in need.
Blessed little memories
Help us bear the cross
And soften all the bitterness
Of failure and loss.
Precious little memories
Of little things we've done
Make the very darkest day
A bright and happy one.*

–HSR

A Meditation

God in His loving and all-wise way
Makes the heart that once was too young yesterday
Serene and more gentle and less restless, too,
Content to remember the joys it once knew. . .
And all that we sought on the pathway of pleasure
Becomes but a memory to cherish and treasure—
The fast pace grows slower and the spirit serene,
And the soul can envision what the eyes have not seen. . .
And so while life's springtime is sweet to recall,
The autumn of life is the best time of all,
For our wild youthful yearnings all gradually cease
And God fills our days with beauty and peace!

–HSR

The Happiness You Already Have

Memories are treasures
That time cannot destroy;
They are the happy pathway
To yesterday's bright joy.

–HSR

Memory Rendezvous

Memory builds a little pathway
That goes winding through my heart.
It's a lovely, quiet, gentle trail
From other things apart.
I only meet when traveling there
The folks I like the best,
For this road I call remembrance
Is hidden from the rest,
But I hope I'll always find you
In my memory rendezvous,
For I keep this little secret place
To meet with folks like you.

–HSR

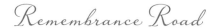

Remembrance Road

There's a road I call remembrance
where I walk each day with you.
It's a pleasant, happy road, my dear,
all filled with memories true.
Today it leads me through a spot
where I can dream awhile,
And in its tranquil peacefulness
I touch your hand and smile.
There are hills and fields and budding trees
and stillness that's so sweet
That it seems that this must be the place
where God and humans meet.
I hope we can go back again
and golden hours renew,
And God go with you always, dear,
until the day we do.

–HSR

Also Known As. . .

He that covereth a transgression seeketh love.
PROVERBS 17:9

Without the ability to remember, we would be like kites with broken strings, floating aimlessly from one breeze to the next. Our memories help us attach our past to our present, and together they form the beginnings of our future. And we have the amazing ability to choose what we remember and what we do not. In a sense, God has given us the ability to sort through our past, keep those things that are precious to us, and push the rest out of the way.

So what memories do you cherish? For most people, friends rank near the top of the "precious" list. It isn't unusual for people to remember their first childhood friend or friends who touched their lives for just a brief time. When friends get together, they often recall the things they did together in the past—their common memories.

Perhaps there is someone in your life, a former friend, who still lingers in your memory. It could be that this friend did something that pulled the two of you apart. You should know that you have the power to restore that friendship, if you choose. Use your God-given ability to keep the good memories and push the bad ones out of the way. Interestingly, this process has an alias—it's also known as forgiveness.

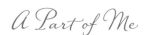

A Part of Me

Dear God, You are a part of me—
You're all I do and all I see;
You're what I say and what I do,
For all my life belongs to You.
You walk with me and talk with me,
For I am Yours eternally,
And when I stumble, slip, and fall
Because I'm weak and lost and small,
You help me up and take my hand
And lead me toward the Promised Land.
I cannot dwell apart from You—
You would not ask or want me to,
For You have room within Your heart
To make each child of Yours a part
Of You and all Your love and care
If we but come to You in prayer.

–HSR

Daily Prayers Dissolve Your Cares

I meet God in the morning
and go with Him through the day,
Then in the stillness of the night
before sleep comes I pray
That God will just take over
all the problems I couldn't solve,
And in the peacefulness of sleep
my cares will all dissolve.
So when I open up my eyes
to greet another day,
I'll find myself renewed in strength
and there will open up a way
To meet what seemed impossible
for me to solve alone,
And once again I'll be assured
I am never on my own.

–HSR

"Thy Will Be Done"

God did not promise sun without rain,
Light without darkness or joy without pain.
He only promised strength for the day
When the darkness comes and we lose our way. . .
For only through sorrow do we grow more aware
That God is our refuge in times of despair,
For when we are happy and life's bright and fair,
We often forget to kneel down in prayer. . .
But God seems much closer and needed much more
When trouble and sorrow stand outside our door,
For then we seek shelter in His wondrous love,
And we ask Him to send us help from above. . .
And that is the reason we know it is true
That bright, shining hours and dark, sad ones, too,
Are part of the plan God made for each one,
And all we can pray is "Thy will be done."
And know that you are never alone
For God is your Father and you're one of His own.

–HSR

Good Morning, God

You are ushering in another day,
untouched and freshly new,
So here I am to ask You, God,
if You'll renew me, too. . .
Forgive the many errors
that I made yesterday,
And let me try again, dear God,
to walk closer in Thy way. . .
But, Father, I am well aware
I can't make it on my own,
So take my hand and hold it tight
for I can't walk alone.

–HSR

He Asks So Little and Gives So Much

What must I do to ensure peace of mind?
Is the answer I'm seeking too hard to find?
How can I know what God wants me to be?
How can I tell what's expected of me?
Where can I go for guidance and aid
To help me correct the errors I've made?
The answer is found in doing three things,
And great is the gladness that doing them brings.
"Do justice"—"Love kindness"—
"Walk humbly with God"—
For with these three things
as your rule and your rod,
All things worth having are yours to achieve,
If you follow God's words
and have faith to believe.

–HSR

Unchangeable Principles

*And God is able to make all grace
abound toward you; that ye, always having
all sufficiency in all things, may
abound to every good work.*
2 CORINTHIANS 9:8

God loves us and it is His desire to bless us abundantly, without measure; He longs to give His children all manner of wonderful gifts. To benefit from these blessings, however, we must open our lives to some of God's unchangeable principles.

Giving versus withholding. God never intended for the blessings He has placed in our lives to remain only with us. They are meant to be passed willingly and joyfully to others.

Laughter versus worry. God's blessings and our worry cannot abide together. Letting go of worry and replacing it with joy and thankfulness can be a daunting task, but it's possible if we made a conscious decision to hand over our worries to God and receive His comfort in return.

Selflessness versus selfishness. Selfishness isolates us, like the child who cannot play with his toys because he is too busy keeping them away from the other children. But when we lay down our treasures, our hands are free to receive new and wonderful gifts from God.

Open your heart to give, to laugh, to share. Honor God's principles and your life will be rich with blessings, friends, and the wonders of God's love.

The Blessings of Patience and Comfort

Realizing my helplessness,
I'm asking God if He will bless
The thoughts you think and all you do
So these dark hours you're passing through
Will lose their grave anxiety
And only deep tranquility
Will fill your mind and help impart
New strength and courage to your heart.
So take the Savior's loving hand
And do not try to understand—
Just let Him lead you where He will,
Through pastures green and waters still,
And though the way ahead seems steep,
Be not afraid for He will keep
Tender watch through night and day,
And He will hear each prayer you pray.

–HSR

In Hours of Discouragement, God Is Our Encouragement

Sometimes we feel uncertain and unsure of everything—
Afraid to make decisions, dreading what the day will bring.
We keep wishing it were possible to dispel all fear and doubt
And to understand more readily just what life is all about.
God has given us the answers, which too often go unheeded,
But if we search His promises, we'll find everything that's needed
To lift our faltering spirits and renew our courage, too,
For there's absolutely nothing too much for God to do. . .
For the Lord is our salvation and our strength in every fight,
Our redeemer and protector, our eternal guiding light.
He has promised to sustain us, He's our refuge from all harms,
And underneath this refuge are the everlasting arms. . .
So cast your burden on Him, seek His counsel when distressed,
And go to Him for comfort when you're lonely and oppressed. . .
For in God is our encouragement in trouble and in trials,
And in suffering and in sorrow He will turn our tears to smiles.

–HSR

No Room for Blessings

Refuse to be discouraged—
refuse to be distressed,
For when we are despondent,
our lives cannot be blessed.
Doubt and fear and worry
close the door to faith and prayer,
And there's no room for blessings
when we're lost in deep despair.
So remember when you're troubled
with uncertainty and doubt,
It is best to tell our Father
what our fear is all about.
For unless we seek His guidance
when troubled times arise,
We are bound to make decisions
that are twisted and unwise.
But when we view our problems
through the eyes of God above,
Misfortunes turn to blessings
and hatred turns to love.

–HSR

God's Tender Care

When trouble comes, as it does to us all
God is so great and we are so small—
But there is nothing that we need know
If we have faith that wherever we go
God will be waiting to help us bear
Our pain and sorrow, our suffering and care—
For no pain or suffering is ever too much
To yield itself to God's merciful touch!

–HSR

There's Peace and Calm in the Twenty-third Psalm

With the Lord as "your Shepherd"
you have all that you need,
For if you "follow in His footsteps"
wherever He may lead,
He will guard and guide and keep you
in His loving, watchful care,
And when traveling in "dark valleys,"
"your Shepherd" will be there. . .
His goodness is unfailing,
His kindness knows no end,
For the Lord is a "Good Shepherd"
on whom you can depend. . .
So when your heart is troubled,
you'll find quiet, peace, and calm
If you'll open up the Bible
and just read this treasured psalm.

–HSR

Faith, Not Feeling

When everything is pleasant and bright
And the things we do turn out just right,
We feel without question that God is real,
For when we are happy, how good we feel. . .
But when the tides turn and gone is the song
And misfortune comes and our plans go wrong,
Doubt creeps in and we start to wonder,
And our thoughts about God are torn asunder—
For we feel deserted in time of deep stress,
Without God's presence to assure us and bless. . .
And it is then when our senses are reeling
We realize clearly it's faith and not feeling—
For it takes great faith to patiently wait,
Believing God comes not too soon or too late.

–HSR

Calm in the Storm

For thou art my rock and my fortress; therefore
for thy name's sake lead me, and guide me.
PSALM 31:3

During His years of ministry here on earth, Jesus' disciples became His closest friends. He had handpicked each one, teaching them about His Father, His kingdom, and His purpose. He regularly rowed out with them on the Sea of Galilee for an evening of fishing and fellowship. These men loved Jesus and were beginning to trust Him as Lord of their lives.

Yet when a violent storm arose on the lake and threatened to swamp the boat, they panicked, fearing loss of life and livelihood. With a word, Jesus rebuked the wind and waves, and the storm subsided! Then, turning to His amazed disciples, He asked, "Where is your faith?"

Are there storms whipping your placid sea into towering waves that threaten to overcome and sink you? So often it's easy to trust Jesus when the skies are clear and the weather fine; but how quickly we are tempted to surrender to fear and doubt when our sea grows restless!

Remember, the same God who calmed the Sea of Galilee can quell any storm that rocks your little boat. He is the same Lord to whom even the winds of adversity and waves of affliction must submit when He says, "Peace. . .be still."

Blessings Come in Many Guises

When troubles come and things go wrong
And days are cheerless and nights are long,
We find it so easy to give in to despair
By magnifying the burdens we bear.
We add to our worries by refusing to try
To look for the rainbow in an overcast sky,
And the blessings God sent in a darkened disguise
Our troubled hearts fail to recognize,
Not knowing God sent it not to distress us
But to strengthen our faith
and redeem us and bless us.

–HSR

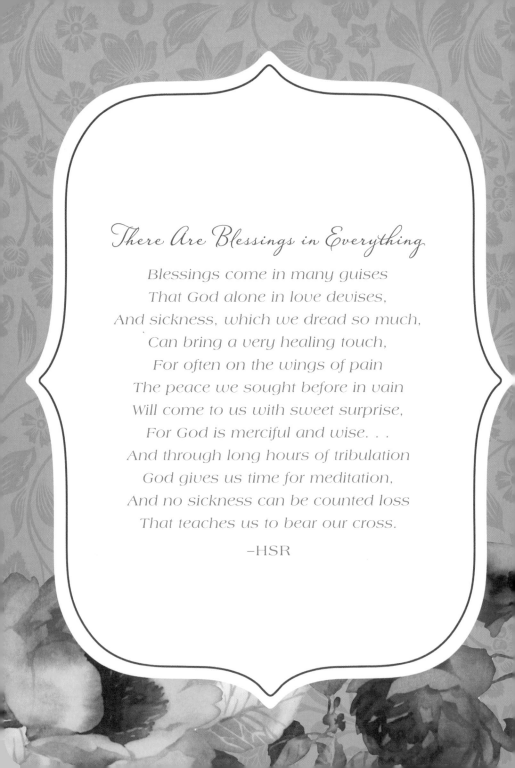

There Are Blessings in Everything

Blessings come in many guises
That God alone in love devises,
And sickness, which we dread so much,
Can bring a very healing touch,
For often on the wings of pain
The peace we sought before in vain
Will come to us with sweet surprise,
For God is merciful and wise. . .
And through long hours of tribulation
God gives us time for meditation,
And no sickness can be counted loss
That teaches us to bear our cross.

–HSR

It Takes the Bitter and the Sweet

Life is a mixture of sunshine and rain,
Laughter and teardrops, pleasure and pain,
Low tides and high tides, mountains and plains,
Triumphs, defeats, and losses and gains,
But always in all ways or some dread affliction,
Be assured that it comes with God's kind benediction,
And if we accept it as a gift of His love,
We'll be showered with blessings
from our Father above.

–HSR

Be Glad

Be glad that your life has been full and complete;
Be glad that you've tasted the bitter and sweet.
Be glad that you've walked in sunshine and rain;
Be glad that you've felt both pleasure and pain.
Be glad that you've had such a full, happy life;
Be glad for your joy as well as your strife.
Be glad that you've walked with courage each day;
Be glad you've had strength for each step of the way.
Be glad for the comfort that you've found in prayer.
Be glad for God's blessings, His love, and His care.

–HSR

Stepping Stones to God

An aching heart is but a stepping stone
To greater joy than you've ever known,
For things that cause the heart to ache
Until you think that it must break
Become the strength by which we climb
To higher heights that are sublime
And feel the radiance of God's smiles
When we have soared above life's trials.
So when you're overwhelmed with fears
And all your hopes are drenched in tears,
Think not that life has been unfair
And given you too much to bear,
For God has chosen you because,
With all your weaknesses and flaws,
He feels that you are worthy of
The greatness of His wondrous love.

–HSR

A Thankful Heart

*Rejoice evermore. Pray without ceasing.
In every thing give thanks: for this is the will
of God in Christ Jesus concerning you.*
1 Thessalonians 5:16–18

She tried her best to stay cheerful. Even when hardships came her way, she hoped to be able to pull off a smile and a song like Paul and Silas did when they were wrongfully locked in a jail cell. *How did those two men find the strength to sing when they were so badly treated?* she wondered.

They surely weren't happy or even cheerful in their hard circumstances, yet they were joyful. Cheer is momentary and can disappear in a flash. Happiness is only a transient thing, but joy is a condition of the heart, the result of being loved and forgiven and in right relationship with God.

You can face trouble with joy in your heart, knowing your heavenly Father is with you. Being thankful for the good and also for what you may define as the bad will allow you to see the blessing in even the most painful situations.

God wants you to experience joy rather than a fleeting moment of happiness. He wants you to revel in the knowledge that you are never alone. He is with you, helping you to find the rainbow in the rain, the sweet honey in the sting of the bee, and the rose among the thorns. Cheerfulness is a precious blessing, but joyfulness gives you the strength to sing even from a jail cell.

Blessings Devised by God

God speaks to us in many ways,
Altering our lives, our plans, and our days,
And His blessings come in many guises
That He alone in love devises,
And sorrow, which we dread so much,
Can bring a very healing touch. . .
For when we fail to heed His voice
We leave the Lord no other choice
Except to use a firm, stern hand
To make us know He's in command. . .
For on the wings of loss and pain,
The peace we often sought in vain
Will come to us with sweet surprise,
For God is merciful and wise. . .
And through dark hours of tribulation
God gives us time for meditation,
And nothing can be counted loss
Which teaches us to bear our cross.

–HSR

There Is a Reason for Everything

God never hurts us needlessly
and He never wastes our pain;
For every loss He sends to us
is followed by rich gain.
And when we count the blessings
that God has so freely sent,
We will find no cause for murmuring
and no time to lament.
For our Father loves His children
and to Him all things are plain;
He never sends us pleasure
when the soul's deep need is pain.
So whenever we are troubled
and when everything goes wrong,
It is just God working in us
to make our spirits strong.

–HSR

Somebody Cares

Somebody cares and always will—
The world forgets, but God loves you still.
You cannot go beyond His love
No matter what you're guilty of,
For God forgives until the end—
He is your faithful, loyal friend. . .
And though you try to hide your face,
There is no shelter anyplace
That can escape His watchful eye,
For on the earth and in the sky
He's ever-present and always there
To take you in His tender care
And bind the wounds and mend the breaks
When all the world around forsakes.
Somebody cares and loves you still,
And God is the Someone who always will.

–HSR

Life

A little laughter, a little song,
A little teardrop
When things go wrong,
A little calm
And a little strife
A little loving
And that is life.

–HSR

How Great the Yield
from a Fertile Field

The farmer plows through the fields of green,
And the blade of the plow is sharp and keen,
But the seed must be sown to bring forth grain,
For nothing is born without suffering and pain,
And God never plows in the soul of man
Without intention and purpose and plan. . .
So whenever you feel the plow's sharp blade,
Let not your heart be sorely afraid,
For like the farmer, God chooses a field
From which He expects an excellent yield. . .
So rejoice though your heart be broken in two—
God seeks to bring forth a rich harvest in you.

–HSR

The Lessons of Love

*For whom the LORD loveth he correcteth;
even as a father the son in whom he delighteth.*

PROVERBS 3:12

When we graduate from school as young adults, we might think we're done with learning. It doesn't take long for us to realize we've just begun! Throughout life, we learn new ways of doing things, delve into new subjects, and discover new ideas. Many of us call ourselves lifelong learners.

In God's school, each one of us is a lifelong learner. No matter how old we are, not one of us can truthfully say we know all we need to know about God's commandments, His Word, or His will. Throughout life, we will stray, we will wander away from Him, and then we will find ourselves right back in front of our Teacher, learners once again. We will never graduate from needing God's correction and guidance, His mercy and forgiveness, until we are standing face-to-face with Him in heaven.

If you are bearing the consequences of a mistake you have made, thank God. Thank God because He cares so much about you that He continues to teach you how to live according to His plan for your life. Thank Him for bringing you to this day, because you have the privilege of rejoicing in His unchangeable truths, gaining spiritual wisdom, and, through your example, teaching others about His love.

Words to Live By

We all need words to live by,
To inspire us and guide us,
Words to give us courage
When the trials of life betide us.
And the words that never fail us
Are the words of God above,
Words of comfort and of courage
Filled with wisdom and with love.

–HSR

Words Can Say So Little

Today is an occasion
for compliments and praise
And saying many of the things
we don't say other days.
For often through the passing days
we feel deep down inside
Unspoken thoughts of thankfulness
and fond, admiring pride.
But words can say so little
when the heart is overflowing,
And often those we love the most
just have no way of knowing
The many things the heart conceals
and never can impart,
For words seem so inadequate
to express what's in the heart.

–HSR

Reward

If you carve your name in a man's heart
With a kindly word and a laugh,
You can be mighty sure that your tombstone
Will be carved with the right epitaph.

–HSR

Everyone Needs Someone

People need people and friends need friends,
And we all need love for a full life depends
Not on vast riches or great acclaim,
Not on success or on worldly fame,
But just in knowing that someone cares
And holds us close in their thoughts and prayers—
For only the knowledge that we're understood
Makes everyday living feel wonderfully good,
And we rob ourselves of life's greatest need
When we lock up our hearts and fail to heed
The outstretched hand reaching to find
A kindred spirit whose heart and mind
Are lonely and longing to somehow share
Our joys and sorrows and to make us aware
That life's completeness and richness depends
On the things we share with our loved ones and friends.

–HSR

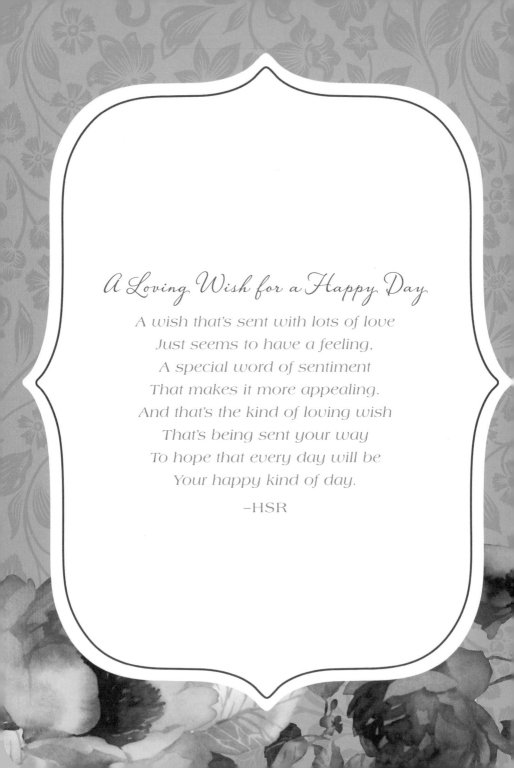

A Loving Wish for a Happy Day

A wish that's sent with lots of love
Just seems to have a feeling,
A special word of sentiment
That makes it more appealing.
And that's the kind of loving wish
That's being sent your way
To hope that every day will be
Your happy kind of day.

–HSR

By All Means Possible

Pleasant words are as an honeycomb,
sweet to the soul, and health to the bones.
PROVERBS 16:24

Amazing advances in technology have made letter writing all but a lost art. Snail mail is used these days primarily for bills, advertisements, and items that can't be easily delivered electronically. But that's exactly why getting a greeting by mail seems so special. It might be a humorous card to brighten the day of a friend who has been going though a tough time. Maybe it's just to say it's been too long since you got together. There are so many reasons not only to speak words of kindness and hope but also to write them down. It's a good idea to have cards on hand, but if you don't, remember it's the message rather than the package. Gracious words, loving words, encouraging words will decorate any plain old piece of paper.

This is a wonderful way to convey your love and devotion to a friend, but certainly not the only way. Take advantage of your email, instant messaging, text messaging, even social networks to let your friends know how much they mean to you.

The Bible is filled with God's words of life and encouragement to us—His friends. It is in fact a letter to us from Him. He loves us so much that He went to the trouble of putting His thoughts into words so we would always know how He feels.

No Favor Do I Seek Today

I come not to ask, to plead or implore You—
I just come to tell You how much I adore You.
For to kneel in Your presence makes me feel blessed,
For I know that You know all my needs best,
And it fills me with joy just to linger with You
As my soul You replenish and my heart You renew.
For prayer is much more than just asking for things—
It's the peace and contentment that quietness brings.
So thank You again for Your mercy and love
And for making me heir to Your kingdom above.

–HSR

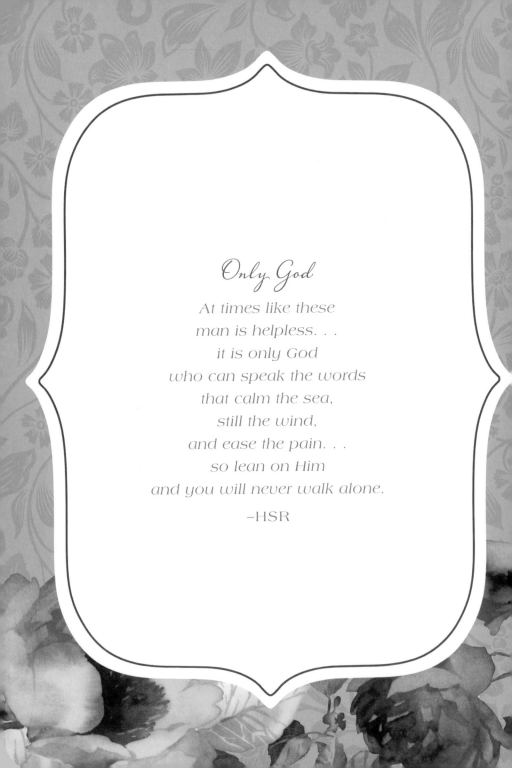

Only God

At times like these
man is helpless. . .
it is only God
who can speak the words
that calm the sea,
still the wind,
and ease the pain. . .
so lean on Him
and you will never walk alone.

–HSR

God Loves Us

We are all God's children
And He loves us, every one.
He freely and completely
Forgives all that we have done,
Asking only if we're ready
To follow where He leads,
Content that in His wisdom
He will answer all our needs.

–HSR

Somebody Loves You

Somebody loves you more than you know,
Somebody goes with you wherever you go,
Somebody really and truly cares
And lovingly listens to all of your prayers. . .
Don't think for a minute that this is not true,
For God loves His children
and takes care of them, too. . .
And all of His treasures are yours to share
If you love Him completely
and show that you care. . .
And if you walk in His footsteps
and have faith to believe,
There's nothing you ask for
that you will not receive!

−HSR

The Heavens Declare the Glory of God

You ask me how I know it's true that there is a living God.
A God who rules the universe—the sky, the sea, the sod—
A God who holds all creatures in the hollow of His hand,
A God who put infinity in one tiny grain of sand,
A God who made the seasons—winter, summer, fall, and spring—
And put His flawless rhythm into each created thing,
A God who hangs the sun out slowly with the break of day
And gently takes the stars in and puts the night away,
A God whose mighty handiwork defies the skill of man,
For no architect can alter God's perfect master plan.
What better answers are there to prove His holy being
Than the wonders all around us that are ours just for the seeing.

–HSR

The Great King

*Great and marvellous are thy works, Lord God
Almighty; just and true are thy ways,
thou King of saints.*
REVELATION 15:3

No nation on earth has ever been ruled by a king like the one
we serve. Unlike other kings who demand service and allegiance,
God rules by serving His citizens from the lowliest to the greatest.
He cares so much for you that He not only will talk with you,
guide you through trials, and help you make decisions, but He
laid down His life for you. He loves us, each one of us, and He
calls us His fellow workers, friends, and children.

God is fair and just in all His rulings. He is true to His Word
and keeps every promise. When has there ever been a ruler,
a king, an elected official like Him? Never! He is completely
honest and wholly infallible. He always chooses what is best for
us and then allows us to make our own choices.

You may not realize that, though He is powerful, He wants
you to stay close to Him so He can bless you and meet your needs.

God reigns with compassion and love, and though He has
no parliament to oversee Him, He needs none. He is great in
power yet, like a loving father, is concerned for you. Doesn't
that make you want to love Him in return? You can count it a
privilege to be a citizen of His eternal kingdom.

Unaware We Pass Him By

On life's busy thoroughfares
We meet with angels unawares,
But we are too busy to listen or hear,
Too busy to sense that God is near,
Too busy to stop and recognize
The grief that lies in another's eyes,
Too busy to offer to help or share,
Too busy to sympathize or care,
Too busy to do the good things we should,
Telling ourselves we would if we could. . .
But life is too swift and the pace is too great,
And we dare not pause, for we might be too late
For our next appointment, which means so much;
We are willing to brush off the Savior's touch.
And we tell ourselves there will come a day
When we'll have more time to pause on our way,
But before we know it, life's sun has set,
And we've passed the Savior but never met.
For hurrying along life's thoroughfare,
We passed Him by but remained unaware
That within the very sight of our eyes,
Unnoticed, the Son of God passed by.

−HSR

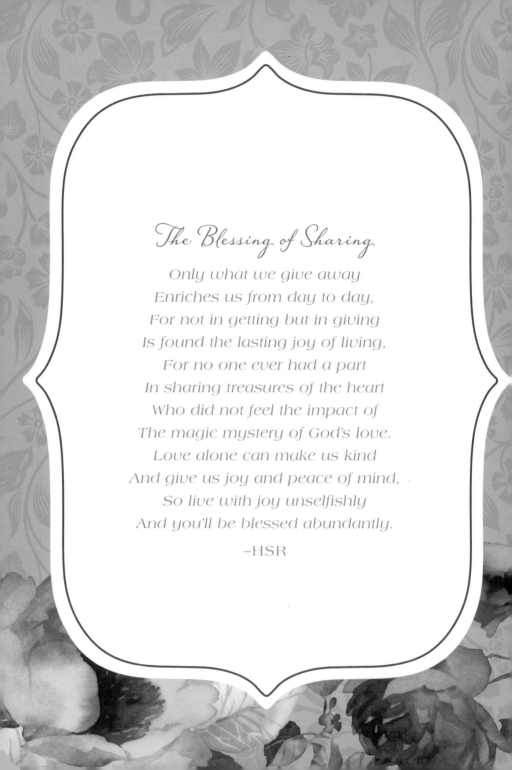

The Blessing of Sharing

Only what we give away
Enriches us from day to day,
For not in getting but in giving
Is found the lasting joy of living,
For no one ever had a part
In sharing treasures of the heart
Who did not feel the impact of
The magic mystery of God's love.
Love alone can make us kind
And give us joy and peace of mind,
So live with joy unselfishly
And you'll be blessed abundantly.

–HSR

Make Me a Channel of Blessing Today

Make me a channel of blessing today—
I ask again and again when I pray.
Do I turn a deaf ear to the Master's voice
Or refuse to hear His direction and choice?
I only know at the end of the day
That I did so little to pay my way.

–HSR

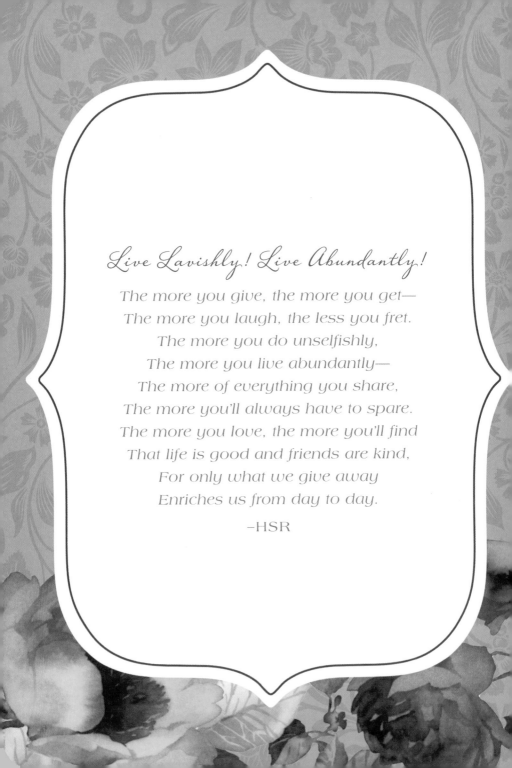

Live Lavishly! Live Abundantly!

The more you give, the more you get—
The more you laugh, the less you fret.
The more you do unselfishly,
The more you live abundantly—
The more of everything you share,
The more you'll always have to spare.
The more you love, the more you'll find
That life is good and friends are kind,
For only what we give away
Enriches us from day to day.

–HSR

Brighten the Corner
Where You Are

We cannot all be famous or listed in *Who's Who*,
But every person, great or small, has important work to do. . .
For seldom do we realize the importance of small deeds
Or to what degree of greatness unnoticed kindness leads. . .
For it's not the big celebrity in a world of fame and praise,
But it's doing unpretentiously in undistinguished ways
The work that God assigned to us, unimportant as it seems,
That makes our task outstanding and brings reality to dreams. . .
So do not sit and idly wish for wider, new dimensions
Where you can put in practice your many good intentions,
But at the spot God placed you, begin at once to do
Little things to brighten up the lives surrounding you. . .
For if everybody brightened up the spot on which they're standing
By being more considerate and a little less demanding,
This dark old world would very soon eclipse the evening star
If everybody brightened up the corner where they are.

–HSR

Finding Enough

*And Elisha said unto her, What shall I do
for thee? tell me, what hast thou in the house?
And she said, Thine handmaid hath not
any thing in the house, save a pot of oil.*
2 KINGS 4:2

Some women really do desire to reach out and touch the lives of others. They see the needs around them and feel the urge to step up and help. Unfortunately, with every idea comes a reason why they aren't able to follow through.

Some may feel they don't have the time and energy necessary after caring for the needs of their own families. Others may believe their homes aren't big enough to host a Bible study or nice enough to invite a lonely neighbor to lunch. Somehow they don't feel they have what it takes to do what God is asking.

Is this the way you feel? Are you concerned that you lack the skills, the talent, the wardrobe, or the stamina to follow through with those things God whispers in your ear? Elisha asked the widow, "What do you have?" She had only a little bottle of oil, but that was all she needed to save her home and children.

When God prompts you to do some act of kindness or calls you to reach out to someone, step out by faith and trust Him to provide. You will soon learn that He never asks you to do anything you are powerless to accomplish. He will take what you have and make it enough.

The Mystery and Miracle of His Creative Hand

In the beauty of a snowflake
falling softly on the land
Is the mystery and the miracle
of God's great, creative hand.
What better answers are there
to prove His holy being
Than the wonders all around us
that are ours just for the seeing?

–HSR

I Meet God in the Morning

Each day at dawning I lift my heart high
And raise up my eyes to the infinite sky.
I watch the night vanish as a new day is born,
And I hear the birds sing on the wings of the morn.
I see the dew glisten in crystal-like splendor
While God, with a touch that is gentle and tender,
Wraps up the night and softly tucks it away
And hangs out the sun to herald a new day. . .
And so I give thanks and my heart kneels to pray,
"God, keep me and guide me and go with me today."

–HSR

Spring Awakens What Autumn Puts to Sleep

A garden of asters in varying hues,
Crimson pinks and violet blues,
Blossoming in the hazy fall,
Wrapped in autumn's lazy pall. . .
But early frost stole in one night,
And like a chilling, killing blight
It touched each pretty aster's head,
And now the garden's still and dead,
And all the lovely flowers that bloomed
Will soon be buried and entombed
In winter's icy shroud of snow. . .
But oh, how wonderful to know
That after winter comes the spring
To breathe new life in everything,
And all the flowers that fell in death
Will be awakened by spring's breath. . .
For in God's plan both men and flowers
Can only reach bright, shining hours
By dying first to rise in glory
And prove again the Easter story.

–HSR

April

April comes with cheeks a-glowing,
Silver streams are all a-flowing,
Flowers open wide their eyes
In lovely rapturous surprise.
Lilies dream beside the brooks,
Violets in meadow nooks,
And the birds gone wild with glee
Fill the woods with melody.

–HSR

The Masterpiece

Framed by the vast, unlimited sky,
Bordered by mighty waters,
Sheltered by beautiful woodland groves,
Scented with flowers that bloom and die,
Protected by giant mountain peaks—
The land of the great unknown—
Snowcapped and towering, a nameless place
That beckons man on as the gold he seeks,
Bubbling with life and earthly joys,
Reeking with pain and mortal strife,
Dotted with wealth and material gains,
Built on ideals of girls and boys,
Streaked with toil, opportunity's banner unfurled
Stands out the masterpiece of art
Painted by the one great God,
A picture of the world.

–HSR

God's True Colors

And God saw every thing that he had made, and, behold, it was very good. And the evening and the morning were the sixth day.

GENESIS 1:31

Picture God holding a palette and a paintbrush. The palette is covered with generous mounds of paint—all the brightest and merriest colors of the universe.

There is the red of a tomato, the purple of a juicy plum, the soft shade of a peach wrapped in its crimson velvet fur, the fresh green of lettuce, the blue of blueberries, the brown speckles of a golden Asian pear, the sweet yellow of pineapple, and the curious purple-black of eggplant.

What if God had made all our fruits and vegetables the same color, size, shape, and texture? Isn't it enough that He feeds us? Isn't it grand of Him to give us such amazing diversity?

What if all the birds were the same, instead of the thousands of species? What if plants and flowers all looked alike? What if there were no bluebonnets, daisies, violets, or Indian paintbrushes, only red roses? What if trees were all covered with the same shade and color leaves, the same bark, and the same-sized branches?

God took great care to design the world beautifully for you. He knew that because you were created in His image you would crave variety and beauty. The uniqueness of all God provided for you shows how much He cherishes you. Why else pomegranate? Why else kiwi?

Where There Is Love

Where there is love the heart is light;
Where there is love the day is bright.
Where there is love there is a song
To help when things are going wrong.
Where there is love there is a smile
To make all things seem more worthwhile.
Where there is love there's a quiet peace,
A tranquil place where turmoils cease.
Love changes darkness into light
And makes the heart take wingless flight.
Oh, blessed are those who walk in love;
They also walk with God above.

–HSR

The Magic of Love

Love is like magic and it always will be,
For love still remains life's sweet mystery.
Love works in ways that are wondrous and strange,
And there's nothing in life that love cannot change.
Love can transform the most commonplace
Into beauty and splendor and sweetness and grace.
Love is unselfish, understanding, and kind,
For it sees with its heart and not with its mind.
Love gives and forgives; there is nothing too much
For love to heal with its magic touch.
Love is the language that every heart speaks,
For love is the one thing that every heart seeks. . .
And where there is love God, too, will abide
And bless the family residing inside.

–HSR

God's Love

God's love is like an island
in life's ocean vast and wide—
A peaceful, quiet shelter
from the restless, rising tide.
God's love is like an anchor
when the angry billows roll—
A mooring in the storms of life,
a stronghold for the soul.
God's love is like a fortress,
and we seek protection there
When the waves of tribulation
seem to drown us in despair.
God's love is like a harbor
where our souls can find sweet rest
From the struggle and the tension
of life's fast and futile quest.
God's love is like a beacon
burning bright with faith and prayer,
And through the changing scenes of life,
we can find a haven there.

–HSR

What Is Love?

What is love? No words can define it—
It's something so great only God could design it.
Wonder of wonders, beyond man's conception—
And only in God can love find true perfection. . . .
For love is unselfish, giving more than it takes—
And no matter what happens, love never forsakes.
It's faithful and trusting and always believing,
Guileless and honest and never deceiving.
Yes, love is beyond what man can define,
For love is immortal and God's gift is divine!

–HSR

Wings of Love

The priceless gift of life is love,
For with the help of God above
Love can change the human race
And make this world a better place. . .
For love dissolves all hate and fear
And makes our vision bright and clear
So we can see and rise above
Our pettiness on wings of love.

–HSR

Be Free!

Now the Lord is that Spirit: and where the Spirit of the Lord is, there is liberty.

2 CORINTHIANS 3:17

Love is meant to take flight! Have you ever noticed how often love is symbolized by things that rise and soar: a bird's wings, a waving banner, the heights of ecstasy, sitting on top of the world?

To be loved is to be raised up out of the mundane, the ordinary, the baseness of our lives. The Bible says that even when we were unlovely God loved us, coming to earth in human form to lift us out of the sin that drags us low, makes us dirty, ashamed, and convinced there is no hope.

Perfect love transforms. . .overwhelming hate, overcoming despair, able to lift a darkened heart bound by loathing, defeat, and fear so it can soar like a feather skipping across the blue dome of the sky.

To grasp that God loves us is freedom from the chains of all those dark and ugly things that would hold us down. Ask Him to remove your fetters and let you rise to the joy of His perfect love. To receive it is to be lifted above hate and fear and anger, to share it with another is to send it fluttering above earthly things to bless and comfort and heal our world.

Not by Chance or Happenstance

Into our lives come many things to break the dull routine—
The things we had not planned or that happen unforeseen—
The unexpected little joys that are scattered on our way,
Success we did not count on or a rare, fulfilling day,
A catchy, lilting melody that makes us want to dance,
A nameless exaltation of enchantment and romance,
An unsought word of kindness, a compliment or two
That set the eyes to gleaming like crystal drops of dew,
The sudden, unplanned meeting that comes with sweet surprise
And lights the heart with happiness like a rainbow in the skies.
Now some folks call it fickle fate and some folks call it chance,
While others just accept it as a pleasant happenstance.
But no matter what you call it, it didn't come without design,
For all our lives are fashioned by the hand that is divine
And every lucky happening and every lucky break
Are little gifts from God above that are ours to freely take.

–HSR

Take Time to Appreciate
God's Blessings

Blessings are all around us.
If we look we can recognize a blessing in
each day, each hour, each minute,
each family member, each friend, each neighbor,
each community, each city, each nation,
each challenge, each word of encouragement,
each flower, each sunbeam, each raindrop,
each awesome wonder crafted by God,
each star, each sea, each bird, each tree,
each sorrow, each disappointment,
each faith, each prayer.

–HSR

Never Despair, God's Always There

In sickness or health,
In suffering and pain,
In storm-laden skies,
In sunshine and rain,
God always is there
To lighten your way
And lead you through darkness
To a much brighter day.

–HSR

Sweet Blessings

Wishing God's sweet blessings
Not in droplets but a shower,
To fall on you throughout the day
And brighten every hour.

–HSR

Look on the Sunny Side

There are always two sides—the good and the bad,
The dark and the light, the sad and the glad. . .
But in looking back over the good and the bad,
We're aware of the number of good things we've had—
And in counting our blessings, we find when we're through
We've no reason at all to complain or be blue. . .
So thank God for the good things He has already done,
And be grateful to Him for the battles you've won—
And know that the same God who helped you before
Is ready and willing to help you once more—
Then with faith in your heart, reach out for God's hand
And accept what He sends, though you can't understand. . .
For our Father in heaven always knows what is best,
And if you trust His wisdom, your life will be blessed. . .
For always remember that whatever betide you,
You are never alone, for God is beside you.

–HSR

Rain On!

When he uttereth his voice, there is a multitude of waters in the heavens, and he causeth the vapours to ascend from the ends of the earth; he maketh lightnings with rain, and bringeth forth the wind out of his treasures.

JEREMIAH 10:13

The rain was a "gully washer," racing along the ditches and off to fill some lake or pond. The thunder rumbled and boomed, and lightning streaked across the dark skies. What do you think about during a heavy rain? Do you wonder if it would be possible to count all the raindrops? How many does it take to quench the thirst of an oak tree, to fill a pond, to refresh the earth?

It would be easier to count the raindrops than to count the blessings God pours out on you every day. Blessings around you go almost unnoticed—the air you breathe, the clouds overhead, the whoosh of the wind in the treetops, the rain itself.

An old hymn says that if the sky were a huge scroll of paper and the ocean filled with ink, it would not be enough to write about all the love God has for us.

Rain—people love the sound of it on the rooftops. We pray for rain to fall on our fields and forests. Next time it rains, watch the drops fall and think of a blessing for each drop. You won't be able to do it, will you? There are so many—so many you cannot fully realize the number—a plethora of blessings every single day. Thank the Lord and let it rain on!

Showers of Blessings

Each day there are showers of blessings
sent from the Father above,
For God is a great, lavish giver,
and there is no end to His love. . .
And His grace is more than sufficient,
His mercy is boundless and deep,
And His infinite blessings are countless—
and all this we're given to keep
If we but seek God and find Him
and ask for a bounteous measure
Of this wholly immeasurable offering
from God's inexhaustible treasure. . .
For no matter how big man's dreams are,
God's blessings are infinitely more,
For always God's giving is greater
than what man is asking for.

–HSR

Beyond Our Asking

More than hearts can imagine or minds comprehend,
God's bountiful gifts are ours without end.
We ask for a cupful when the vast sea is ours,
We pick a small rosebud from a garden of flowers,
We reach for a sunbeam but the sun still abides,
We draw one short breath but there's air on all sides.
Whatever we ask for falls short of God's giving,
For His greatness exceeds every facet of living,
And always God's ready and eager and willing
To pour out His mercy, completely fulfilling
All of man's needs for peace, joy, and rest,
For God gives His children whatever is best.
Just give Him a chance to open His treasures,
And He'll fill your life with unfathomable pleasures—
Pleasures that never grow worn out and faded
And leave us depleted, disillusioned, and jaded—
For God has a storehouse just filled to the brim
With all that man needs, if we'll only ask Him.

–HSR

Climb till Your Dream
Comes True

Often your tasks will be many,
and more than you think you can do.
Often the road will be rugged,
and the hills insurmountable, too.
But always remember, the hills ahead
are never as steep as they seem,
And with faith in your heart, start upward
and climb till you reach your dream.
For nothing in life that is worthy
is ever too hard to achieve
If you have the courage to try it
and you have the faith to believe.
For faith is a force that is greater
than knowledge or power or skill,
And many defeats turn to triumphs
if you trust in God's wisdom and will.
For faith is a mover of mountains—
there's nothing that God cannot do—
So start out today with faith in your heart
and climb till your dream comes true.

–HSR

The Bend in the Road

Sometimes we come to life's crossroads
and view what we think is the end,
But God has a much wider vision,
and He knows it's only a bend.
The road will go on and get smoother,
and after we've stopped for a rest,
The path that lies hidden beyond us
is often the part that is best.
So rest and relax and grow stronger,
let go and let God share your load,
And have faith in a brighter tomorrow;
you've just come to a bend in the road.

–HSR

Wish Not for Ease
or to Do as You Please

If wishes worked like magic
and plans worked that way, too,
And if everything you wished for,
whether good or bad for you,
Immediately were granted
with no effort on your part,
You'd experience no fulfillment
of your spirit or your heart.
For things achieved too easily
lose their charm and meaning, too,
For it is life's difficulties
and the trial times we go through
That make us strong in spirit
and endow us with the will
To surmount the insurmountable
and to climb the highest hill.
So wish not for the easy way
to win your heart's desire,
For the joy's in overcoming
and withstanding flood and fire,
For to triumph over trouble
and grow stronger with defeat
Is to win the kind of victory
that will make your life complete.

–HSR

The Greatness of Love

And I will make them and the places round
about my hill a blessing; and I will cause
the shower to come down in his season;
there shall be showers of blessing.
EZEKIEL 34:26

What is the most amazing thing that has happened during your lifetime so far? Perhaps you were awed when Neil Armstrong set foot on the moon in 1969; when Dr. Robert Jarvik implanted the first artificial heart in 1982; when you realized you could talk to anyone, anywhere, on a device no larger than the palm of your hand! These and other advances in medicine and technology happened and continue to happen because people use the power of their imaginations and put them to work.

When we attempt to describe what God is like, however, the power of our imagination falls woefully short. That's because no matter how big our idea may be, we cannot begin to grasp His limitless love or His infinite power. When we try, we limit our ability to reach out as far as He would have us reach, to believe in the blessings He has in mind for us, and to recognize all the opportunities He has placed right in front of us.

God invites you to ask Him for whatever you can dream and then let Him take care of the rest. His imagination and power are far greater than anything you could think of, so prepare to be amazed at how much more your heavenly Father will choose to shower on you!

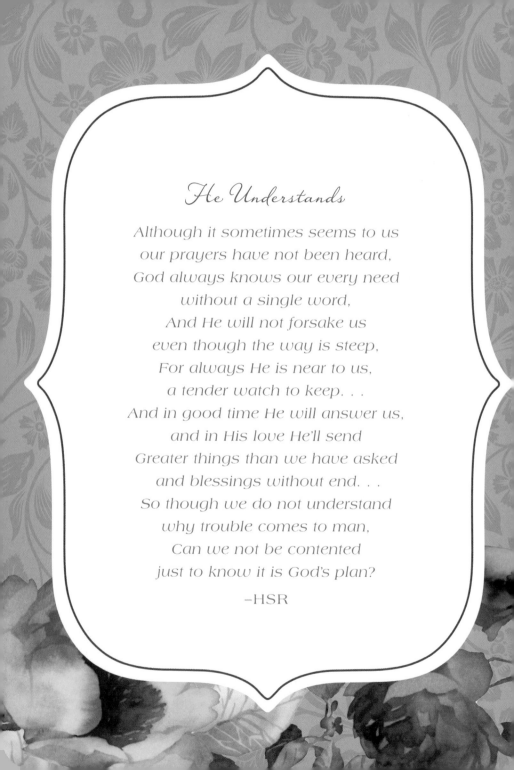

He Understands

Although it sometimes seems to us
our prayers have not been heard,
God always knows our every need
without a single word,
And He will not forsake us
even though the way is steep,
For always He is near to us,
a tender watch to keep. . .
And in good time He will answer us,
and in His love He'll send
Greater things than we have asked
and blessings without end. . .
So though we do not understand
why trouble comes to man,
Can we not be contented
just to know it is God's plan?

–HSR

God's Stairway

Step by step we climb each day
Closer to God with each prayer we pray,
For "the cry of the heart" offered in prayer
Becomes just another "spiritual stair"
In the "heavenly staircase" leading us to
A beautiful place where we live anew. . .
So never give up for it's worth the climb
To live forever in "endless time"
Where the soul of man is safe and free
To live in love through eternity!

–HSR

What More Can You Ask?

God's presence is ever beside you,
as near as the reach of your hand.
You have but to tell Him your troubles—
there is nothing He won't understand. . .
And knowing God's love is unfailing,
and His mercy unending and great,
You have but to trust in His promise,
"God comes not too soon or too late". . .
So wait with a heart that is patient
for the goodness of God to prevail,
For never do prayers go unanswered,
and His mercy and love never fail.

–HSR

We Can't, but God Can

Why things happen as they do
we do not always know,
And we cannot always fathom
why our spirits sink so low.
We flounder in our dark distress;
we are wavering and unstable,
But when we're most inadequate,
the Lord God's always able—
For though we are incapable,
God's powerful and great,
And there's no darkness of the mind
God cannot penetrate. . .
And while He may not instantly
unravel all the strands
Of the tangled thoughts that trouble us,
He completely understands—
And in His time, if we have faith,
He will gradually restore
The brightness to our spirits
that we've been longing for. . .
So remember there's no cloud too dark
for God's light to penetrate
If we keep on believing
and have faith enough to wait.

–HSR

Not What You Want
but What God Wants

Do you want what you want when you want it?
Do you pray and expect a reply?
And when it's not instantly answered
Do you feel that God passed you by?
Well, prayers that are prayed in this manner
Are really not prayers at all,
For you can't go to God in a hurry
And expect Him to answer your call.
For prayers are not meant for obtaining
What we selfishly wish to acquire,
For God in His wisdom refuses
The things that we wrongly desire. . .
Wake up! You are missing completely
The reason and purpose of prayer,
Which is really to keep us contented
That God holds us safe in His care.
And God only answers our pleadings
When He knows that our wants fill a need,
And whenever our will becomes His will,
There is no prayer that God does not heed!

–HSR

Waiting on God

But my God shall supply all your need according to his riches in glory by Christ Jesus.
PHILIPPIANS 4:19

Standing in line, sitting in traffic, pacing in front of the microwave, waiting for your computer to boot up or the doctor to call. Perhaps you enjoy the pause such situations create, but most people see them as a waste of time and a source of irritation.

Not all waiting is a waste of time, however. When you are waiting and watching for an answer to prayer, God is giving you a chance to wait on Him, to be seated for a few minutes in His throne room. He may feel you need time to think about what you have asked for and how it will impact your life. He may be giving you an opportunity to see another point of view or correct an error in your own thought process. Or God may feel that a "pregnant" pause is a good way to impress on you the true value of the answer He is sending your way.

Waiting on God is one of the most blessed places you can be as His child. During that time, you are focused on His presence and His priorities, poised to listen for His voice. If you find yourself in a place of waiting on God, see the experience as a gift in itself and cherish every moment.

Remember This

Great is the power of might and mind,
But only love can make us kind,
And all we are or hope to be
Is empty pride and vanity.
If love is not a part of all,
The greatest man is very small.

–HSR

The World Would Be a Nicer Place
if We Traveled at a Slower Pace

Amid stresses and strain, much too many to mention,
And pressure-packed days filled with turmoil and tension,
We seldom have time to be friendly or kind,
For we're harassed and hurried and always behind. . .
And while we've more gadgets and buttons to press,
Making leisure time greater and laboring less,
And our standards of living they claim have improved
And repressed inhibitions have been freed and removed,
It seems all this progress and growth is for naught,
For daily we see a world more distraught. . .
So what does it matter if man reaches his goal
And gains the whole world but loses his soul?
For what have we won if in gaining this end
We've been much too busy to be kind to a friend?
And what is there left to make the heart sing
When life is a cold and mechanical thing?
And are we but puppets of controlled automation
Instead of joint heirs to God's gift of creation?

–HSR

The World Needs Friendly Folks Like You

In this troubled world it's refreshing to find
Someone who still has the time to be kind,
Someone who still has the faith to believe
That the more that you give, the more you receive,
Someone who's ready by thoughts, word, or deed
To reach out a hand in the hour of need.

–HSR

The Gift of Lasting Love

Love is much more than a tender caress
And more than bright hours of happiness,
For a lasting love is made up of sharing
Both hours that are joyous and also despairing.
It's made up of patience and deep understanding
And never of stubborn or selfish demanding
It's made up of climbing the steep hills together
And facing with courage life's stormiest weather.
And nothing on earth or in heaven can part
A love that has grown to be part of the heart
And just like the sun and the stars and the sea,
This love will go on through eternity,
For true love lives on when earthly things die,
For it's part of the spirit that soars to the sky.

–HSR

A Pattern for Living

"Love one another as I have loved you"
May seem impossible to do,
But if you will try to trust and believe,
Great are the joys that you will receive.
For love makes us patient, understanding, and kind,
And we judge with our hearts and not with our minds,
For as soon as love entered the heart's open door,
The faults we once saw are not there anymore—
And the things that seem wrong begin to look right
When viewed in the softness of love's gentle light
For love works in ways that are wondrous and strange,
And there is nothing in life that love cannot change,
And all that God promised will someday come true
When you love one another the way He loved you.

–HSR

Loving Others

*And walk in love, as Christ also hath loved us,
and hath given himself for us an offering and a
sacrifice to God for a sweetsmelling savour.*
EPHESIANS 5:2

Responses to a natural disaster such as a hurricane demonstrate the compassion and desire to help others that God has placed within each of us. You've doubtless seen it at the scene of a house fire or the search for a missing child. Some volunteers give money, some build homes, and others give their blood to help those in need.

It is in this way that we see how we are created in God's image, for He is full of compassion and lovingkindness. Jesus set the ultimate example by giving up His place in heaven and coming to earth to rescue us from the penalty of our disobedience. While He was here, He did more than redeem us; He also ministered to the many and various needs of the people He encountered. He reached out to the poor, orphans, widows, the sick, and the disabled. Jesus loved even those who didn't recognize Him, and He fought for everyone, even those who could not return the favor.

What can you do today to show your love for God and your concern for others? How can you live a life of love, like Christ did? You must know someone who could use some encouragement or a helping hand. Reach out with all the compassion and kindness God has placed within you.

A Thankful Heart

Take nothing for granted, for whenever you do,
The joy of enjoying is lessened for you.
For we rob our own lives much more than we know
When we fail to respond or in any way show
Our thanks for the blessings that daily are ours—
The warmth of the sun, the fragrance of flowers,
The beauty of twilight, the freshness of dawn,
The coolness of dew on a green velvet lawn,
The kind little deeds so thoughtfully done,
The favors of friends and the love that someone
Unselfishly gives us in a myriad of ways,
Expecting no payment and no words of praise.
Oh, great is our loss when we no longer find
A thankful response to things of this kind.
For the joy of enjoying and the fullness of living
Are found in the heart that is filled with thanksgiving.

–HSR

Things to Be Thankful For

The good, green earth beneath our feet,
The air we breathe, the food we eat,
Some work to do, a goal to win,
A hidden longing deep within
That spurs us on to bigger things
And helps us meet what each day brings—
All these things and many more
Are things we should be thankful for. . .
And most of all, our thankful prayers
Should rise to God because He cares.

–HSR

Thank You, God, for Everything

Thank You, God, for everything—the big things
and the small—For every good gift comes from God,
the giver of them all, And all too often we accept
without any thanks or praise the gifts God sends
as blessings each day in many ways. And so at this
time we offer up a prayer to thank You, God,
for giving us a lot more than our share.
First, thank You for the little things that often come
our way—the things we take for granted and don't
mention when we pray—the unexpected courtesy,
the thoughtful, kindly deed, a hand reached
out to help us in the time of sudden need.
Oh, make us more aware, dear God, of little daily
graces that come to us with sweet surprise from
never-dreamed-of places. Then thank You for the
miracles we are much too blind to see, and give us
new awareness of our many gifts from Thee.
And help us to remember that the key to life
and living Is to make each prayer a prayer of
thanks and each day a day of thanksgiving.

–HSR

So Many Reasons
to Love the Lord

Thank You, God, for little things that come unexpectedly
To brighten up a dreary day that dawned so dismally.
Thank You, God, for sending a happy thought my way
To blot out my depression on a disappointing day.
Thank You, God, for brushing the dark clouds from my mind
And leaving only sunshine and joy of heart behind.
Oh God, the list is endless of the things to thank You for,
But I take them all for granted and unconsciously ignore
That everything I think or do, each movement that I make,
Each measured, rhythmic heartbeat, each breath of life I take
Is something You have given me for which there is no way
For me in all my smallness to in any way repay.

–HSR

This Is All I Ask

Lord, show me the way
I can somehow repay
The blessings You've given to me. . .
Lord, teach me to do
What You most want me to
And to be what You want me to be. . .
I'm unworthy I know
But I do love You so—
I beg You to answer my plea. . .
I've not got much to give
But as long as I live
May I give it completely to Thee!

–HSR

Forever Thanks

Give thanks for the blessings
That daily are ours––
The warmth of the sun,
The fragrance of flowers.
With thanks for all the thoughtful,
Caring things you always do
And a loving wish for happiness
Today and all year through!

–HSR

Just a Word

*A word fitly spoken is like apples of gold
in pictures of silver.*
PROVERBS 25:11

A card in the mail, a pat on the back from your boss, a smile from your spouse, or a "Great supper, Mom!" from your teenager warms your heart and encourages you. Such small acts of gratitude have a positive effect on a person. A word of gratitude changes our attitudes toward work and people. Do you know how gratitude feels from the giving side?

Do you show gratitude for all God has done for you? The men healed by Jesus were so thrilled by what they had received that they rushed off without saying thank You, and that was so wrong. Jesus commended only the one who returned to thank Him.

We should always notice the hand of God in our lives and see to it that we tell Him how much we appreciate His goodness and faithfulness to us. Such generosity from a fellow human being would surely evoke thanks from us. Do we forget the Lord because we can't see Him? Are we blinded to His wonders because of our busy schedules?

Spend some time each day noticing His gifts and thanking Him. He does not change, and His attitude doesn't need improvement, but giving thanks does the giver as much good as the receiver. You are sure to be changed as you stop to say, "Thanks, God."

About the End

And now that you've come to the end of this book,
Pause and reflect and take a swift backward look
And you'll find that to follow God's commandment each day
Is not only the righteous and straight, narrow way,
But a joyous experience, for there's many a thrill
In going God's way and in doing His will. . .
For in traveling God's way you are never alone,
For all of your problems God takes as His own,
And always He's ready to counsel and guide you,
And in sadness or gladness He's always beside you. . .
And to live for God's glory and to walk in His truth
Brings peace to the angel and joy to the youth,
And at the end of life's journey, there's His promised reward
Of life everlasting in the house of the Lord.

–HSR

About the Author

Born in Ohio in 1900, Helen Steiner Rice began writing at an early age. In 1918, Helen took a job at a public utilities company, eventually becoming one of the first female advertising managers and public speakers in the country. At age 29, she married banker Franklin Rice, who committed suicide in 1932, never having recovered mentally and financially from losses incurred during the Great Depression. Following her husband's death, Helen used her gift of verse to encourage others. Her talents came to the attention of the nation when her greeting card poem "The Priceless Gift of Christmas" was read on the Lawrence Welk Show. Soon a series of poetry books, a source of inspiration to people worldwide, followed. Helen died in 1981, leaving a foundation that offers assistance to the needy and elderly.